# THE REMNANT CHURCH

Mark T. Barclay

All scripture references are quoted from the
*King James Version* of the Holy Bible
unless otherwise noted.

Second Edition
First Printing 1998


ISBN 0-944802-32-X

Write:
Mark Barclay Ministries
P.O. Box 588, Midland, MI 48640-0588

# CONTENTS

A Word From the Author

Introduction

# A WORD FROM THE AUTHOR

The author realizes the principles of hermeneutical laws and that some of the scriptures here literally relate to the Jew and the church in their own parts. However, he also realizes that the principles are repetitive in each generation and therefore applicable for today. Even today, God is taking care of His remnant. Just as the Church was an addition to the Jew, the Protestant to the Catholic, the Pentecostal to the Protestant, the Charismatic to the Pentecostal, the Word of Faith to the Charismatic, so will this new remnant be to the rest.

# INTRODUCTION

I am writing this book to stir up hunger in the Body of Christ for the move of God's Spirit. God has progressively breathed from His nostrils a divine breath of magnitude force which hits planet earth like a rushing, mighty wind. I suppose God will never stop this process until He climaxes the ages.

Therefore, we must consistently be in line with God so that we are the ones who enjoy His revivals and His outpourings. Someone always does; it should be us. And it can be you, my friend, if you don't let tradition, doctrinal dogma, or personal pride hinder your reception. God wants you, personally, to be part of this next wave of His glory. Get in line for it! Pray for it! Watch for it! It's beginning to touch down even now.

# CHAPTER 1
# A POWERFUL RIVER OF GOD

In September of 1987, at Ed Dufresne's Healing Center dedication service, the hand of the Lord came upon me and opened a window and revealed to me a vision—one that relates (I believe) to the end-time revival.

I saw a vision of God's throne. I didn't see the Person on it, but coming out of the heart of that big throne—that big, king-like chair—was something like a fragrance. It was like an essence that was coming out, and it came out from God. It became heavy, and it fell down to this floor. This floor was like a mirror, reflecting everything. It was shiny and smooth all around the throne. As this fragrance left God and fell on this floor, it turned into a really gooey, really thick honey-like substance, and it just kind of rolled out over the floor. There was an edge to this floor in front of the throne of God, and this substance flowed out over the edge of it. I felt sweet inside. It began to fall from Heaven onto the earth, and as it fell, it thickened. The farther it fell from the throne onto earth, the more it picked up momentum and speed until it was a powerful momentum with magnificent speed like that of a falling weight. It fell with magnitude force by the time it hit the earth, like a glass of water being poured on an ant. I couldn't see to the left or to the right or behind me.

Something else I saw . . . by the time it entered the earth's atmosphere, it turned into a molten, lava-like substance, like from a volcano, and it covered everything. I watched it in this vision the Lord gave me in a visitation. I watched this molten, lava-like substance coming from God that just consumed the whole earth. I saw little things (that's the only way I can define them), and they represented the people of this earth and the things of this earth. Some were black, and some were white with black spots on them. I saw this molten, lava-like substance cover everything and everyone. No one was exempt. People ran from it, and it just engulfed them. (God spoke to me and defined it to me later.)

Some opened their arms and received it, and it just flowed right over the top of them. When I looked, all I saw were fumes coming off this lake of molten-like stuff on the face of the earth. Then I began to see that there were bumps as this river came—it was like a flood, a flash flood. I wondered, Why can't I stop this flood? But there was no answer. It just came so fast. It was like a flood; people were running. Some didn't know about it; some were scared. It just covered everything.

There were some who were so overtaken by this that they seemed like mere bumps. God spoke to me and said, "The bumps are those people who curse Me. This fire will just consume them, and it'll be their end."

Then I saw others, and as I watched, first their fingertips and then their hands raised. These little bumps began to burst through this molten-like lava, and I noticed that the ones who were spotted came out white and clean as snow and began to stand up in the midst of this river. The Spirit of the Lord said, "There will be no more curse for these.

There will be no more sickness for these. There will be no more disease for these. These will be the powerful ones. These will be the holy ones. These will be the ones who are wrapped in white garments and thoroughly cleansed by the flow of God."

The Lord spoke to me and said, "The bumps—the dark, black things you saw when this molten lava covered the earth—were the ones who were in opposition; they were Christ rejectors. They had turned against the Church. They had been fooling themselves and telling themselves that they could be saved by their yesterday-works or by their money or by the things that they possessed or by their maneuvers or by their friends or by some other means." But they seemed cursed by God. This river of God engulfed them, and it was their end. They were terminated, and they were ready for Judgment Day. Then God said, "These are those who curse Me and curse My men, and they shall be no more!"

Then the Lord said, "The white ones who were all spotted were the Church—the people who were having struggles and yet they loved God. They were having struggles and yet they loved—oh, so much loved Jesus and wanted freedom from their sin, freedom from their torment, freedom from the things that lay behind them."

How many of you even today who read this book have some things, or a list of things, you wish could just be purged out of your mouth and out of your head and out of your heart?

That's what those white spotted bumps were. They represented people who were white and spotted. As this molten, lava-like flow from God, like a refiner's fire, went

3

over the top of the Church and those who were not cursing God or standing against God, they began to raise their hands up out of that furnace-like flow. As they stood, I saw that there were no more spots. They were pure and shiny, and it almost hurt my eyes to look upon them.

God began to say, "That's the flow that's now proceeding out of My throne room. I have saved the best for last— My fragrance, My very essence! The glory of the Lord is coming and protruding out of My Spirit, out of My heart right now, and it's landing on the throne room floor." That is the stage in which I see the Church. The Heavenly Father's fragrance is in that thick honey-like flow. It's the very essence of God.

You know, I was thinking about this on the airplane coming home the other day. It seems so significant that it was honey in Heaven and a consuming fire on the earth. It was sweet and gooey as honey on the floor of Heaven, but down here it was an uncontrollable, engulfing flow of purifying substance. It alarmed me that no one, not one person on all the earth in this vision that I saw—this visitation— escaped it.

The Lord said, "Warn My people. Prepare them, for if they are in line, it won't catch them like a thief in the night. It will purify them. It will strengthen them, and they will rise up in what I promised them." But the ones who are running from God purposely and the ones who are just denying God and the ones who hate God and the ones who curse the preachers and curse the churches—I tell you, folks, it wouldn't surprise me if all of them and all the worldly media were swallowed up in this river. It wouldn't surprise me if some of the organizations that are crooked and mean and taking advantage of widows and all those promoting pornography were just engulfed. I believe that is what the Lord was trying to tell me.

I asked God, "In what stage is this now? Where is the front of this most powerful wave?" God answered, "It is just now on the throne room floor."

That's right. This river, right now, is just in the stage of landing on the floor of God. It hasn't come over the edge yet. In fact, drips of it are just starting to come over the edge. Drip, drip, drip—that's where we see a little revival here and a little revival there, like fresh oil from Heaven.

We are preaching revival, but we haven't really seen it yet. You're feeling it a little bit. How many of you are feeling a little bit of newness and freshness and strength? It's coming upon us. How many are a little bit afraid of it? Is anyone afraid of it? I am! I tremble at it, yet I hunger for it. I want to be involved in it so much. Listen, when that river hits earth, when that honey-like flow hits earth, it's going to be like fire, and you won't escape it. It will either consume you (if you're resisting and cursing God), or you will be purified by it (if you're hungering, thirsting, and chasing after God). I don't think you'll pull anyone out of it. In fact, some may even pull you into it. Either way, you'll end up in it!

This is why we need to print books. This is why we need our own printing presses. This is why we need airplanes. This is why we need larger buildings. This is why we need more preachers working for the ministry. This is why we need to send people to the mission field. Humanity is suffering and hurting, and we're in the gospel work. I think if we're not careful, both preachers and even believers will lose track of our commission and simply become ones who come to feast, and we'll be feeding nobody! The greater one is the one who feeds, the one who supplies, the one who provides. That's our blessing on this earth, to store up treasures in Heaven by toiling in this life.

How many of you just want to obey God—that's what's in your heart? Let's just stop here and pray in the Spirit. Maybe you wish to meditate on what I've just told you.

"Include us, Lord. Put us in, Lord Jesus. Help us, Lord Jesus, to be part of what You're doing in this hour. Glory be to God!"

The Bible talks about a river coming out of the throne of God. It's a wonderful river, one that flows right from God's heart. In it there is life and blessing. Read about it here in Revelation 22:1-3:

> *"And he shewed me a pure river of water of life, clear as crystal, proceeding out of the throne of God and of the Lamb.*
>
> *In the midst of the street of it, and on either side of the river, was there the tree of life, which bare twelve manner of fruits, and yielded her fruit every month: and the leaves of the tree were for the healing of the nations.*
>
> *And there shall be no more curse: but the throne of God and of the Lamb shall be in it; and his servants shall serve him . . ."*

I believe that God wants us all to be full of His Spirit. He wants us to walk in His fullness. It is God's intention to encourage us and strengthen us so we can do His work even more faithfully.

6

I yearn to be in this constant flow of God. I know with all that is within me that God is about to pour out of His Spirit like never before. I know without a doubt that the vision I've shared with you is God's revelation to us. The word goes out to all who listen and give their attention.

Don't be one of those who looks at it, judges it, puts it on trial, or shelves it. Prepare now. Get ready. Get your swimming clothes on. God is going to open His floodgates.

Go right into the next chapter of this book. I want to share with you about revival and the five "Ms" of history. "Catch the wave!"

# CHAPTER 2
# HISTORY REPEATING ITSELF

## CATCH THE WAVE

*"Behold, I and the children whom the LORD hath given me are for signs and for wonders in Israel from the LORD of hosts, which dwelleth in mount Zion."*

Isaiah 8:18

*"Ask ye of the LORD rain in the time of the latter rain; so the LORD shall make bright clouds, and give them showers of rain, to every one grass in the field."*

Zechariah 10:1

*"And it shall come to pass, that every one that is left of all the nations which came against Jerusalem shall even go up from year to year to worship the King, the LORD of hosts, and to keep the feast of tabernacles.*

*And it shall be, that whoso will not come up of all the families of the earth unto Jerusalem to worship the King, the LORD of hosts, even upon them shall be no rain.*

*And if the family of Egypt go not up, and come not, that have no rain; there shall be the plague, wherewith the LORD will smite the heathen that come not up to keep the feast of tabernacles."*

Zechariah 14:16-18

9

*"Be patient therefore, brethren, unto the coming of the Lord. Behold, the husbandman waiteth for the precious fruit of the earth, and hath long patience for it, until he receive the early and latter rain.*

*Be ye also patient; stablish your hearts: for the coming of the Lord draweth nigh."*

James 5:7-8

There is a powerful wave of God's Spirit now moving across the land. It's like a gigantic cloud full of God's greatness and His best. It's a glory cloud. It's a cloud of power which will deliver, heal, charge, and challenge the people of the earth. The powers of darkness will melt and run off like a stream of debris flowing away from believers as though driven by a mighty wind.

The remnant of God's people will be pure and awesome in power. Their behavior alone will put a great fear and trembling in the hearts of the wicked. There has never been anything like it; neither will there ever be again.

God will be right in the midst of them. They will be filled with God's glory, love, forgiveness, and sweetness. Many people will be attracted to these Christians who resemble God.

Some will call it a revival! This won't be wrong. A revival it will be, yet it will be so powerful that it will be considered and remembered as more than a revival. A revival is simply this: people coming to sit once again at the feet of Jesus, hungering and thirsting for Him, and Jesus obliging them.

You see, people serve the Lord to such a degree that they soon find themselves consumed with their visions, goals, projects, programs, doctrines, and even each other. Without even purposing it, they have lost track of Jesus, Himself. They soon begin to quarrel, divide, and get restless. Their programs become dull and unsatisfying and begin to fail.

Revival is when we stir up our hunger and thirst and go back to the Bible basics and God meets us there.

Revival is always twofold: (1) Man hungering, thirsting, and drawing nigh to God, and (2) God feeding, giving drink, and drawing nigh to man.

When man and God draw nigh to each other, it is the most powerful, most demonstrative union in all creation. God loves man. God loves man to be godly.

## HISTORY REPEATING ITSELF

As far back as you can trace, God has made attempts to speak to and walk with man. With each attempt came a remnant response. Only a portion of mankind would listen. Only a few would obey.

We can rapidly think of some of the more modern examples. What about the Pentecostal outpouring of Azusa Street? People prayed and fasted for an outpouring. They were dry and dull; they knew a refreshing was a must. God heard their cry and poured out of His Spirit. The result is what we call the Pentecostal movement of our day.

The unforgettable issue here is that only certain people would have anything to do with this revival. Many people, including some of those who prayed for it, stood against it. Only a remnant moved on in God. Some still stand against it today. Some say it is of the devil.

It wasn't too many years after this great outpouring that the Pentecostal people began once again to pray. The remnant now seemed like a multitude. Doctrines and traditions were of utmost importance. Some of the major leadership went home to Heaven, and others lost their fame, as even others marched on and clung to their revival.

God heard the cry once again from His people and poured out of His Spirit. What a notable outpouring it was! We call it the Charismatic movement. It went from a few hungry Pentecostals to an overwhelming amount of people from all religious walks. It revolutionized the world. Sad to say, though, some stood against it and wouldn't go with it. In its early years, only a few (a remnant) went with it and enjoyed it. Many people, including those who prayed it in, stood against it. Many do, even today.

History once again repeated itself. The movement grew to astronomical stages. Thousands and thousands of people belonged to it and enjoyed it. But when the Spirit wind stopped blowing, men began to quarrel and divide themselves, and the great remnant (now a multitude) was thirsty once again.

God repeated Himself again when He breathed on the prayer warriors and the frontliners. They rose up and began to inhale the life of the Lord. The results? The Word of Faith movement was on the go. God began to do some tremendous things. A few (a remnant) sought it out and clung to it. They were persecuted and mocked; some were even rejected by their own. They rode it out, and the wave proved powerful enough for many people.

Of course, some did and still do stand against it; but

the remnant is enjoying every bit of it.

Now listen, friends. Sooner or later this faith revival will begin to wane. History will probably repeat itself. Many are now beginning to thirst for more and hunger for fresh manna. God will answer them. A new wave of His Spirit is coming. It most definitely will be the greatest yet.

And where will we find you, my friend? In the multitude, with the persecutors or dogmatic ones? Will we find you hungering and thirsting after righteousness? Will some of you Word of Faith brothers repeat history and stand in opposition of this outpouring? Will you refuse to change or be changed?

It will come upon us rapidly and overtake the remnant. Will you be in line for it when it comes?

## A CLOUD OF DARKNESS

Of course, we all know that satan will not allow this to happen without a fight. You can count on there being counterfeits and counter moves. If God is going to pour out His grace, satan will pour out his darkness. Thank God for Romans 5:20, "Where sin abounded, grace did much more abound."

Listen friend, if a wave of God's glory and God's gifts is coming upon us, then the devil will put a wave of his darkness upon the earth. God's wave will overcome and swallow up satan's wave. God's wave will manifest on His remnant. Satan's wave will probably manifest on the rest.

> *"For, behold, the darkness shall cover the earth, and gross darkness the people . . ."*
>
> Isaiah 60:2

13

The cloak of darkness is now beginning to hover over the earth. It's like a deep fog. It blurs the vision and disorientates the human compass. People get lost in it, and it breeds fear. There seems to be no end to it. It is covering the whole earth. They call it AIDS, cancer, despair, gloom, etc. Only the glorious light of Christ can shine through it. I'm going to keep my light burning. How about you?

Gross darkness will cover the people. Gross to me means maximum, no room for more. This is already happening. People (even some Christian people) are snared and have been enticed by pornography, perverted sexual acts, extreme abuse of drugs, alcohol, and the like. Suicide and murder are partners in this darkness.

Years ago it was reported to me that a young man from a Christian home had committed perverted sex acts with his pet animal. Another reported that a man had raped his almost infant daughter. Listen to me! If this isn't gross darkness, I don't know what it is. I wish I could say that no Christian anywhere is caught up in any of these things, but I cannot. God will put His glory upon the remnant, and they will overcome. Are you part of it?

## THE FIVE "Ms"

Many of us have heard of the five Ms. These five words, all starting with the letter M, define to us repetition throughout history. Here's what they are:

### MESSAGE

*God has always had a message for the human race. He has spoken to each generation that had ears to hear and prophets to speak. God even has a message today in our complex society.*

## MAN

*God chose man to speak to and deal with man. I suppose God could have chosen anything He wanted to, but He chose man. Even Jesus came to mankind in the form of a man. God has always taken His message and delivered it to the human race through man.*

## MOVEMENT

*As God's message is proclaimed through this man or small group of men, it causes what we call a movement. God uses this movement's momentum to spread the word mouth to mouth. The message spreads rapidly, and we have a revival on our hands. Praise God!*

## MONUMENT

*God has always had a problem with man. Man always wants to build a temple, tabernacle, or monument. We do this even today. We have monumental pastors with monumental churches. I cannot understand why we all think big means best. Certainly big churches mean more money and more equipment and more buildings. But does big always spell order, success, obedience, excellence, etc.? No, it does not! We have taken pastors of large denominations, and we have monumentalized them. That's right. We have monumental churches, monumental ministries, monumental ministers with monumental names, and we even have monumental doctrines. They get bigger and bigger, and Jesus gets smaller and smaller.*

*Now wait a minute. I don't think big is bad, either. Big or small isn't the issue here. The issue is exaltation. Who and what are being promoted and exalted?*

## MORTUARY

*As these monumental things of our movement grow out of proportion, things begin to stagnate and stink. That's right. I've watched it and so have you.*

*There is nothing more ridiculous than to see an average believer pretend he is a Moses, a Northern preacher have a Texas accent, or a small-town pastor have a metropolitan vision. But because we all think big is best, we worship, bow down to, and chase after the big. I wonder if we will ever learn.*

Every movement ends in disarray, and it slowly smothers out the revival fires. Of course, some stay very loyal to it, and they push it along while God moves on.

Let's not let these five Ms repeat themselves. We can stop them now. Don't let the stench and grip of traditionalism bog you down.

Break away from the "mortuary" phase, and catch the wave!

# CHAPTER 3
# AS IN THE DAYS OF NOAH

## A DESTRUCTION IS DETERMINED

*"Now it will come about in that day that the remnant of Israel, and those of the house of Jacob who have escaped, will never again rely on the one who struck them, but will truly rely on the LORD, the Holy One of Israel.*

*A remnant will return, the remnant of Jacob, to the mighty God.*

*For though your people, O Israel, may be like the sand of the sea, Only a remnant within them will return; A destruction is determined, overflowing with righteousness."*

Isaiah 10:20-22 (NAS)

I believe we each have a choice to make that can change our destiny. Jesus also taught us this as He predicted end-time conditions. I don't believe God wants anyone to live outside of grace or to be willingly disobedient.

God wants each of us to be part of His remnant—those people who are hungering, thirsting, and chasing after Him.

Judgment, darkness, famines, and destructions will hit planet earth. The good news is that the remnant will be overflowing with righteousness. I look at it this way. There are two sides—darkness versus light, good versus bad, sweet versus bitter, pains of destruction versus fruits of righteousness.

## OVERFLOWING WITH RIGHTEOUSNESS

Right in the midst of poverty and lack will be plenty. The unjust will have empty barns, and the just will have full barns. The remnant will be clean, not dirty; healed, not sick; sweet, not bitter. They will have upright mouths, not be gossips; good reputations, not bad reputations; consecrated lifestyles, not permeated with the world, the flesh, and the devil.

God honors right-living. God rewards diligent seekers. God answers righteous men's prayers.

Wonderful and glorious streams of righteousness will override and overflow the dark streams of the world.

Chase after God and be in the line for reward, blessing, deliverance, and God's portion for you.

Stay out of sin and worldly living. You'll just end up jealous and mad at the remnant people. You'll just end up in trouble with God and perhaps find yourself at the wrong judgment place.

Listen, friend. You've got to beat the devil. Fight off his trickery and walk as uprightly as you can. God will do the rest.

## THE LORD WILL RISE UPON YOU

*"Arise, shine; for your light has come, and the glory of the LORD has risen upon you.*

*For behold, darkness will cover the earth, and deep darkness the peoples; But the LORD will rise upon you, and His glory will appear upon you.*

*And nations will come to your light, and kings to the brightness of your rising.*

*Lift up your eyes round about, and see; They all gather together, they come to you. Your sons will come from afar, and your daughters will be carried in the arms.*

*Then you will see and be radiant, and your heart will thrill and rejoice; Because the abundance of the sea will be turned to you, the wealth of the nations will come to you.*

*A multitude of camels will cover you, the young camels of Midian and Ephah; All those from Sheba will come; They will bring gold and frankincense, and will bear good news of the praises of the LORD."*

Isaiah 60:1-6 (NAS)

This is it. Catch that wave! God's glory is rising upon us. We won't have to muster it up, pray it through, or borrow it from another. It will rise upon us, and it will be bright with light and quite glorious.

*"For behold, darkness will cover the earth, and deep darkness the peoples . . . "*

Isaiah 60:2 (NAS)

This is one reason the remnant will be so bright and outstanding. I predict that very gross sin and fleshly behavior will consume people. The result of this wickedness will cause great diseases and the transmittal of foul things, *but* God's people will be overcomers and powerful adversaries to these dark happenings.

> *"But the Lord will rise upon you, and His glory will appear upon you. And nations will come to your light . . . "*

That's it, friend. Remember it. God is going to get on us. God will be recognized on us. God will draw people to us. Nations (people) will come to our light, not our sinful nature but our light. Praise God, I can hardly wait!

## KNOWING BOTH SIDES

God instructed me several months ago to both warn His people of the darkness, decay, and destruction that are coming as well as reveal the things of the new revival. We've got to know both sides.

By now, you have noticed that I have written this book in that fashion. I am trying to warn you of the dark side while showing you the bright side.

Everyone will say they are or want to be part of the remnant. I tell you, friend, a great call is going out to every Christian, but only a remnant will have ears to hear. Only a remnant will respond.

## AS IN THE DAYS OF NOAH

Listen to what Jesus said:

> *"But of that day and hour no one knows, not even the angels of heaven, nor the Son, but the Father alone.*

*For the coming of the Son of Man will be just like the days of Noah.*

*For as in those days which were before the flood they were eating and drinking, they were marrying and giving in marriage, until the day that Noah entered the ark,*

*and they did not understand until the flood came and took them all away; so shall the coming of the Son of Man be."*

Matthew 24:36-39 (NAS)

It would be hard to deny that the days we live in are, in fact, like the days of Noah. Jesus said here in these verses that people did not even understand what hour they lived in until Noah went into the ark.

Listen folks, only a remnant was saved from all humanity. In fact, only eight people were saved. Some think they were rescued because they were relatives of God's man. Surprise! They were saved because they refused to carry on like the people of their day. Instead they built and worked on God's project. This has got to be similar to this hour we live in.

I don't believe there will be any tagalongs or relative salvations. I believe that each and every person must choose salvation and work out this salvation with fear and trembling. We must be found working and worshipping and serving in order to enter in.

Let's examine the days of Noah. Jesus said they were eating, drinking, marrying, and giving in marriage. I guess simply said, they chose the lust of the flesh and the cares of this world rather than the Kingdom's reproach.

## EATING

*I believe people today are snared by their appetites. I don't mean table food as much as I do the spirit of the thing. Even in church life, people seem to want fellowship and socializing over prayer and preaching. They want home meetings instead of congregational meetings; the feeling is to have a personal touch and time for each other. Who has time to build the Church unless it be the remnant?*

## DRINKING

*To me, this represents looseness, mockery, soulful delights, and flighty- and party-like attitudes. Many Christians today hate authority, and they hate strong leadership. Many want to cut back on church-related items so there is more time to celebrate and make noise and what they call "rejoice." Don't let this thing get on you, or you will not show up to the ark one day.*

## MARRYING

*I believe it is God's plan for us to be married and have children and live in a family setting. But today, too many people, even Christians, take these vows too lightly. Many leave their spouses because of "incompatibility" or some other excuse. I'm not judging victims of divorce, and I don't necessarily preach against remarriage, but I do think we should try to show some moderation in these areas of life. Let's not be found like the woman at the well who had wasted five husbands and now doesn't even bother with the ceremony.*

## GIVING IN MARRIAGE

*To me, this is the most scary one because I believe it fits us today. I like to explain it this way. Many people are not only married, but they have given themselves totally over to the marriage, the home, and the kids.*

*Now we all know that the marriage won't work if we never give ourselves to it, but many people are slaves to it. They would like to work in the church or the ministry, but their spouse wants them home, their kids need them, or their grass needs to be mowed. On goes the story.*

*I believe too much togetherness is as bad as too little. Most of us don't need more time with spouse and kids as much as we need to improve what time we do have with them. Better quality, not more quantity.*

*One man said he had to quit serving as an usher in the church because his kids needed him. The pastor reminded him that the last thing his kids needed was more of him. He was gossiping, had a bad attitude, and seldom worshipped the Lord.*

*This pastor told him what his kids needed was more of Jesus. They needed more Bible teaching and more Sunday school. They needed to see their mommy and daddy laughing, weeping, kneeling, bowing, jumping, and dancing in God's house.*

*Guard yourself so you are not the one holding your husband or wife from seeking the Lord. Remember, your kids are watching you at church and at home.*

*Listen friend, the grass will wait, the house will wait, the sports and hobbies will wait. Go for God.*

*Why is it people always choose church days and times to do other things?*

*What is wrong with Monday, Tuesday, Friday, and Saturday nights? Why Sunday or midweek service times?*

They were eating, drinking, marrying, and giving in marriage. They gave into the worldly lusts and lost track of the seriousness of the hour. So shall the coming of the Son of Man be.

## THE 50 PERCENT FACTOR

I suppose a lot of people will disagree with this portion of the book. Many people teach or believe in a live-any-way-you-want-to grace.

I think there is something here we should at least look at. It must be here for a reason.

*"Then shall two be in the field; the one shall be taken, and the other left.*

*Two women shall be grinding at the mill; the one shall be taken, and the other left.*

*Watch therefore: for ye know not what hour your Lord doth come.*

*But know this, that if the goodman of the house had known in what watch the thief would come, he would have watched, and would not have suffered his house to be broken up.*

*Therefore be ye also ready: for in such an hour as ye think not the Son of man cometh."*

Matthew 24:40-44

TWO MEN – Two men in the field. One is taken, and one is left. One from two is 50 percent.

TWO WOMEN – Two women will be at the mill working together. One will go; one will be left. One from two is 50 percent.

> *"Then shall the kingdom of heaven be likened unto ten virgins, which took their lamps, and went forth to meet the bridegroom.*
>
> *And five of them were wise, and five were foolish.*
>
> *They that were foolish took their lamps, and took no oil with them:*
>
> *But the wise took oil in their vessels with their lamps.*
>
> *While the bridegroom tarried, they all slumbered and slept.*
>
> *And at midnight there was a cry made, Behold, the bridegroom cometh; go ye out to meet him.*
>
> *Then all those virgins arose, and trimmed their lamps.*
>
> *And the foolish said unto the wise, Give us of your oil; for our lamps are gone out.*
>
> *But the wise answered, saying, Not so; lest there be not enough for us and you: but go ye rather to them that sell, and buy for yourselves.*
>
> *And while they went to buy, the bridegroom came; and they that were ready went in with him to the marriage: and the door was shut.*

*Afterward came also the other virgins, saying, Lord, Lord, open to us.*

*But he answered and said, Verily I say unto you, I know you not.*

*Watch therefore, for ye know neither the day nor the hour wherein the Son of man cometh."*

Matthew 25:1-13

TEN VIRGINS – Five ran out of oil just before the bridegroom came. While they went for more oil, the bridegroom came and took away the five that had oil. Five went; five were left. Five from ten is 50 percent.

Let's look a little closer at this parable of the ten virgins. Of course, we can automatically say that a literal interpretation fits the Jew and the Church, but I just wonder if it fits somewhere else as well.

Check this out:
- 10 virgins
- All had lamps; all lamps were burning.
- All had oil; 5 (50 percent) had extra oil.
- All virgins were waiting for the bridegroom's arrival.
- All lamps were burning until the final hour.
- All virgins heard the bridegroom announcement.
- 5 virgins cry for help.
- 5 lamps begin to go out.
- 5 virgins with oil refuse to lend oil.

- 5 virgins without oil go for more oil, and while they are gone, the 5 virgins with extra oil go to the marriage feast.

- 5 others return to that place with oil, asking to come in. They are told no. The Lord did not know them.

- 5 (50 percent) with full-blaze lamps *went.*

- 5 (50 percent) with flickering lamps *were left behind.*

*This little light of mine*

*I'm going to let it shine.*

*This little light of mine*

*I'm going to let it shine.*

*Let it shine, let it shine, let it shine!*

## STRAIGHT AND NARROW IS THE WAY

*"Enter ye in at the strait gate: for wide is the gate, and broad is the way, that leadeth to destruction, and many there be which go in thereat:*

*Because strait is the gate, and narrow is the way, which leadeth unto life, and few there be that find it."*

Matthew 7:13-14

I wonder how often (in our advertising campaigns) we tell people the real truth about Heaven and hell. It seems to me that we have really squeezed open the gates and put a few bends in the road. Sometimes I am shocked at how people (Christians) live and even more shocked that ministers don't seem to do much about it.

The gate and way to destruction is wide and broad. The gate and way to Heaven is narrow, and it is straight.

Many will go in at the broad gate—the easy way.

Only a few (a remnant) will find the way to salvation. It is straight and narrow.

# CHAPTER 4
# A DIVINE SEPARATION

## JUDGMENT IS COMING TO THE HOUSE OF GOD

*"For the time is come that judgment must begin at the house of God: and if it first begin at us, what shall the end be of them that obey not the gospel of God?*

*And if the righteous scarcely be saved, where shall the ungodly and the sinner appear?"*

1 Peter 4:17-18

God's judgment is just, and it only brings forth fruit which is righteous. God comes to us in question form to place His judgment upon us. He approaches us and says something like this: "You have been letting your mouth run wild; won't you fix it immediately? You have been cheating on your tithes and offerings; won't you please begin to give again? You have been looking at the wrong things; won't you please fix your eyes on Me again? You have been meditating in the wrong things; won't you please meditate in My Word? You have been hanging around the wrong people; won't you please come out from among them and separate yourself?"

This is how God's judgment comes to His house. All we have to do is admit sin and confess it. He is faithful and just to not only forgive us of that sin, but to cleanse us from all unrighteousness. We will be better and cleaner people because of it.

Don't be disobedient to the gospel. This opens doors for the enemy to come in and steal from you, kill you or someone of yours, and destroy what you are or what you have.

Now here is the danger. The devil's judgment is a wicked and cruel judgment. He simply ransacks your life. I don't believe he can do this if we obey God and allow God to judge us. However, I do know that the devil is just waiting for you to deny self-judgment or God's convictions—then he's got you.

Don't let it happen to you!

Listen friend, I am not teaching here that only a God-selected, elite group will enter God's mercy and grace. What I am telling you is that there are too many scriptures warning us to walk uprightly for us to ignore them.

## ONCE SAVED—ALWAYS SAVED

I hope so! I know that God spent a lot to get us saved and wishes for all men to come to full repentance.

A man came to me once and confessed that he had committed a foul sin, a perverted sexual act, with another. When I dealt with him about it, he simply said, "Well, I may have lost some of my blessings down here because I did this sin, but I know God doesn't judge me, and everything will be okay in Heaven." He kind of grinned and hit me with eternal security doctrines. I told him if he wanted to believe that, it was his business, but he had better stop living like he believed it.

Hey, there are just too many times in the Bible where we are warned about wrong-living. Let's be as clean and as righteous as we can. Even then God will have to help us. We can't be righteous on our own.

## CLEAN HANDS AND CLEAN HEART

*"Who may ascend into the hill of the LORD? And who may stand in His holy place?*

*He who has clean hands and a pure heart, who has not lifted up his soul to falsehood, and has not sworn deceitfully.*

*He shall receive a blessing from the LORD and righteousness from the God of his salvation.*

*This is the generation of those who seek Him, who seek Thy face—even Jacob."*

Psalm 24:3-6 (NAS)

God's enemies laugh at Him when you willfully sin. Both God and the devil know when you fall into temptation and when you betray Christ through premeditated sin.

You and I will do enough damage, not even meaning to. Let's not sit around with scorners, stand around with scoffers, and listen to wicked counseling.

## HATING THE WORK OF EVILDOERS

*". . . I will walk within my house in the integrity of my heart.*

31

*I will set no worthless thing before my eyes; I hate the work of those who fall away; It shall not fasten its grip on me."*

Psalm 101:2-3 (NAS)

Watch out! There are backsliders, Christ rejecters, and mockers everywhere. They are desperately trying to contaminate you and victimize you.

Watch out! They have the venom of serpents on their lips, and they want to get it on yours. They are arrogant troublemakers. They are suspicious and strike like weasels.

Be careful that you don't hate the person. Hate the evil that they do. "I hate the work of those who fall away." Hate it! Despise it! It is shameful, and only satan enjoys it.

Be careful! This well-designed evil will try to fasten its grip on you. "It shall not fasten its grip on me."

God's remnant will reach out to hurting and suffering people but in justice, not sympathy. They will respond biblically, not soulfully.

Listen, friend. Those who fall away have some of the most juicy and dramatic stories you have ever heard. They will get your juices flowing if you don't guard yourself. They always seem right, but they live wrong.

## ONLY THE FAITHFUL

*"My eyes shall be upon the faithful of the land, that they may dwell with me; He who walks in a blameless way is the one who will minister to me."*

Psalm 101:6 (NAS)

I love all people, and I believe God wants to help everyone. *But* I am not going to allow unfaithful, ill-behaved people to minister to me—not even in my helps staff. I am constantly believing God for people to become faithful so I can have them work in His house.

I am on a diligent search for blameless people, those who despise sin and wallow only in righteousness. Of course, I will minister to everyone. It is just that I want people who minister to me to be clean and in right standing with God.

God is looking for a few good men to lead the powerful force—the Church.

## THE SOULFUL CHURCH

Let me comment here on the days of Noah again, because the same behavior patterns are found today. Jesus said it would be this way.

Many, many Christians today want to be saved and be led by soulful leaders. They want to be petted and patted. They want to be touched and rubbed. They want to be politicked and manipulated. They dream of fantasies, and they love socializing. Some even smoke and drink and carouse around.

"We want fellowship," they cry. They want outings, picnics, and barbeques. They want short church services, plenty of music to stimulate them, and mini-sermons that are sweet and palatable.

They want to be emotionally stimulated and have a good time. If we priests don't fulfill their cravings, they simply abandon us, call us names, and go somewhere else. Oh, God, we need a revival so desperately.

## A DIVINE SEPARATION

*"Another parable put he forth unto them, saying, The kingdom of heaven is likened unto a man which sowed good seed in his field:*

*But while men slept, his enemy came and sowed tares among the wheat, and went his way.*

*But when the blade was sprung up, and brought forth fruit, then appeared the tares also.*

*So the servants of the householder came and said unto him, Sir, didst not thou sow good seed in thy field? from whence then hath it tares?*

*He said unto them, An enemy hath done this. The servants said unto him, Wilt thou then that we go and gather them up?*

*But he said, Nay; lest while ye gather up the tares, ye root up also the wheat with them.*

*Let both grow together until the harvest: and in the time of harvest I will say to the reapers, Gather ye together first the tares, and bind them in bundles to burn them: but gather the wheat into my barn."*

Matthew 13:24-30

- Wheat and tares – both harvested.
- Wheat for master's use.
- Tares to be piled and burned.
- Both were in same field.
- One sown by God.

- One sown by enemy.
- Christians told not to separate.
- Some tares look and act like wheat.
- Some wheat look and act like tares.
- God separates them.

*"When the Son of man shall come in his glory, and all the holy angels with him, then shall he sit upon the throne of his glory:*

*And before him shall be gathered all nations: and he shall separate them one from another, as a shepherd divideth his sheep from the goats:*

*And he shall set the sheep on his right hand, but the goats on the left.*

*Then shall the King say unto them on his right hand, Come, ye blessed of my Father, inherit the kingdom prepared for you from the foundation of the world:*

*For I was an hungred, and ye gave me meat: I was thirsty, and ye gave me drink: I was a stranger, and ye took me in:*

*Naked, and ye clothed me: I was sick, and ye visited me: I was in prison, and ye came unto me.*

*Then shall the righteous answer him, saying, Lord, when saw we thee an hungred, and fed thee? or thirsty, and gave thee drink?*

*When saw we thee a stranger, and took thee in? or naked, and clothed thee?*

*Or when saw we thee sick, or in prison, and came unto thee?*

*And the King shall answer and say unto them, Verily I*

*say unto you, Inasmuch as ye have done it unto one of the least of these my brethren, ye have done it unto me.*

*Then shall he say also unto them on the left hand, Depart from me, ye cursed, into everlasting fire, prepared for the devil and his angels:*

*For I was an hungred, and ye gave me no meat: I was thirsty, and ye gave me no drink:*

*I was a stranger, and ye took me not in: naked, and ye clothed me not: sick, and in prison, and ye visited me not.*

*Then shall they also answer him, saying, Lord, when saw we thee an hungred, or athirst, or a stranger, or naked, or sick, or in prison, and did not minister unto thee?*

*Then shall he answer them, saying, Verily I say unto you, Inasmuch as ye did it not to one of the least of these, ye did it not to me.*

*And these shall go away into everlasting punishment: but the righteous into life eternal."*

Matthew 25:31-46

- Sheep and goats together.
- Both are harvested.
- Sheep on right; goats on left.
- Sheep will be saved.
- Goats get eternal punishment.
- Determined by what they did and didn't do.
- God separated.

*"Then shall the kingdom of heaven be likened unto ten virgins, which took their lamps, and went forth to meet the bridegroom.*

*And five of them were wise, and five were foolish.*

*They that were foolish took their lamps, and took no oil with them:*

*But the wise took oil in their vessels with their lamps.*

*While the bridegroom tarried, they all slumbered and slept.*

*And at midnight there was a cry made, Behold, the bridegroom cometh; go ye out to meet him.*

*Then all those virgins arose, and trimmed their lamps.*

*And the foolish said unto the wise, Give us of your oil; for our lamps are gone out.*

*But the wise answered, saying, Not so; lest there be not enough for us and you: but go ye rather to them that sell, and buy for yourselves.*

*And while they went to buy, the bridegroom came; and they that were ready went in with him to the marriage: and the door was shut.*

*Afterward came also the other virgins, saying, Lord, Lord, open to us.*

*But he answered and said, Verily I say unto you, I know you not.*

*Watch therefore, for ye know neither the day nor the hour wherein the Son of man cometh."*

Matthew 25:1-13

Please re-read the previous portion of this book called "The 50 Percent Factor."

> *"I charge thee therefore before God, and the Lord Jesus Christ, who shall judge the quick and the dead at his appearing and his kingdom;*
>
> *Preach the word; be instant in season, out of season; reprove, rebuke, exhort with all longsuffering and doctrine.*
>
> *For the time will come when they will not endure sound doctrine; but after their own lusts shall they heap to themselves teachers, having itching ears;*
>
> *And they shall turn away their ears from the truth, and shall be turned unto fables."*
>
> 2 Timothy 4:1-4

- Some will not put up with sound doctrine.
- Hirelings and paid teachers will pile up.
- People will run to them to have their itch scratched.
- These teachers will be numerous (piled up).
- Many will turn their ears from the truth.
- They will turn aside to myths.
- They will seek to fill their own desires.
- I call the services of these people and teachers "goat gatherings."

There are more Bible examples warning us of things to come. Let's be aware of satan's attacks and his trickery.

Let me remind you that satan does not come to you in a red Halloween mask with horns and a pitch-forked tail. Most of the time he is going to come to you as an angel.

That's right! In fact, he's coming not only as an angel but an angel of light—in disguise. Disguise and trickery are his specialties.

> *"And no marvel; for Satan himself is transformed into an angel of light.*
>
> *Therefore it is no great thing if his ministers also be transformed as the ministers of righteousness; whose end shall be according to their works."*
>
> 2 Corinthians 11:14-15

Be sure your "discerner" is working properly. Be sure you are aware of satan's activities and whereabouts. Don't let him take you out of the race.

You and I must put our foot down. We must put a stop to sin. We must do all we can to live clean, pure, unspotted lives. Do your best, and God will aid you.

Submit to leaders who are clean and fruitful. If you know for sure that you are connected with someone who is in adultery or fornication or such sins, do your best to separate yourself.

You must be separated from darkness and sin. You must be free from fellowshipping with sinners and sitting with scornful people.

Remember, most of us sin enough accidentally to keep us repenting and confessing constantly. Please don't ever purpose to sin.

# CHAPTER 5
# I PREDICT

I predict a separation will take place right here in our time. It just may be divinely ordered. Hirelings and teachers will be piled up, and they will be easy to find—plenteous. They will teach things that will be pleasing and tickling to the ears of those who run to them. (The remnant will have nothing to do with them.) They will have soft, friendly smiles and almost mushy voices. They will draw soulful people by the thousands. It will be like bees to sugar.

These men will do no, or very little, correcting and rebuking. There will be little or no warning in their messages. They will permit sin in their camps and allow people to live however they wish.

People who have itches will run to these flesh mongrels for a scratch. It will be carnal and pretentious.

Along with these people who have itchy ears will be the truth rejecters and those who will not put up with sound doctrine.

I call these meetings "goat gatherings." I predict there will be goat gatherings in cities and counties all over the nation.

I predict the sheepfolds with God-appointed shepherds will also be in these cities. They will be less flamboyant and much more stable. They will be clean and strong and well groomed. Their pastors will be holy and honest men, speaking the truth in love, rebuking, correcting, instructing, and guarding the flock.

I predict there will be a divine separation as God prepares to climax the ages. There will be goat gatherings with hirelings leading them, and there will be the remnant.

## A REMNANT WILL RETURN

*"The remnant shall return, even the remnant of Jacob, unto the mighty God."*

Isaiah 10:21

I believe this remnant of God's people will be most powerful. They will come out from every rank and gathering. They will return to a mighty God.

God is about His most powerful business of all history. People who walk with God in these last days will be awesome.

God will be the only thing on their mind. There will be absolutely nothing that will stop them. They will be a powerful, demonstrative force. God will walk with them every waking moment.

## SIGNS AND WONDERS

*"Behold, I and the children whom the LORD hath given me are for signs and for wonders in Israel from the LORD of hosts, which dwelleth in mount Zion."*

Isaiah 8:18

This remnant will be constantly and quite consistently demonstrating God's power and His Spirit. There will be very unusual things happening. Awesome miracles and manifestations will take place as God Himself walks with the few.

I saw in the spirit a very unusual vision. I saw a lady in a grocery store doing her weekly shopping. She was part of this remnant. God spoke to her by His Spirit and instructed her to give her cart a push and let it go quickly down the aisle and smash into another lady's cart. She did it! (The remnant will be obedient.) The cart smashed into the other one, and a baby flew into the air and landed back into the cart. A mother came for her baby screaming and shouting and holding her child in her arms.

The lady that pushed the cart now had arrived at the crash site. She was beginning to feel bad for what she did, but the child's mother began to scream even louder. As the words could be understood, she was yelling out shouts of victory, for her child was made whole. She was shouting, "My baby! My baby! She had no feet and she was deformed, but when your cart hit my cart, she was totally made whole."

I predict that great and powerful things will happen at the hand of the Holy Spirit. Believers will be amazed at how God uses them to demonstrate His power in these days, *but* with their amazement will come a great reverence for God in their midst. This will cause a greater and greater hunger, and believers everywhere will be coveting the best gifts for their life and ministry.

We are about to see the most demonstrative move of God that has ever happened. Not only will people be miraculously healed, but there will be other great signs.

Believers will prophesy, and men will come to the altars of the Lord weeping and repenting. This will cause revival fires in the realm of evangelism. Many, many people will turn into soul-winners. Many people will be saved.

Probably among the greatest of all signs will be the cleanliness of the Church. Even now as I write this book, God is fixing and cleaning us up. Like night and day—so will be the difference between the Church and the world. Just our purity and holiness will be an awesome threat to the rest of mankind.

God is going to purge His Church from every filthy thing. We will be free from things like malice, malicious gossip, talebearing, and strife. The remnant Church will be closely knit together. A real unity of purpose will grip the Church, and God's work will be accelerated.

A tremendous healing wave will be swooping over the Church. There will be many unusual and extraordinary miracle healings—in the church services and outside the church—by the hands of believers. We will witness an awesome move of healing virtue. There will be sicknesses and diseases that will be diagnosed as having no cure. Only the blood of Jesus and the ministry of His believers will be able to free people from these things. The Church itself will suffer less and less. We will be free from the addiction to medicine that now grips so many.

A wonderful and glorious deliverance will take place in the midst of the Church. Those who are tormented by demons will run to the remnant Church for freedom and liberty. The practice of casting out demons will be common. The word of this will spread, and the Church will become a purging house for those who are bound. The Church itself will be delivered and set free from antagonizing bad habits and fleshly practices. God will cleanse the believers, and they will rejoice and be filled with glee.

The ministry gifts will demonstrate tremendous altar services. God will work with them in the most unique way—a way that will excite the Church and a way that will differentiate between God's men and false prophets.

There will be a very sweet taste in the mouth of believers. A clean, fresh fragrance will enhance the worship of the saints. Believers will feel clean and renewed, and God will be pleased.

# CHAPTER 6
# THE MOST MAGNIFICENT
# OUTPOURING

## A NEW REVIVAL

*"I will surely assemble, O Jacob, all of thee; I will surely gather the remnant of Israel; I will put them together as the sheep of Bozrah, as the flock in the midst of their fold: they shall make great noise by reason of the multitude of men.*

*The breaker is come up before them: they have broken up, and have passed through the gate, and are gone out by it: and their king shall pass before them, and the LORD on the head of them."*

Micah 2:12-13

I truly believe that this prophet, Micah, had a revelation of the Church. I also believe that the principles here fit what God is saying to us today. This is God's will for His Church.

## ASSEMBLE TOGETHER

*"I will surely assemble, O Jacob, all of thee . . ."*

Micah 2:12

What a contrast. While many people are crying to go home, quit, or shorten the church services, the remnant is shouting for more. We have to be careful not to forsake the assembling of ourselves together as the manner of some is, *but* so much the more as we see the day of the Lord coming upon us. (See Hebrews 10:25.)

God is instructing us to come together more often and for longer periods of time.

Things will get so bad in the world that Christians will have to run to church daily to be rekindled and to be strengthened.

Mark my words!

## A REMNANT

*". . . I will surely gather the remnant of Israel . . ."*

Micah 2:12

Listen, friend, I'm not saying that God will choose and point out some to be with Him and some to go to damnation. Our lifestyle, our confession, our yielding to His Spirit, our obedience to the gospel, etc., will automatically categorize us. You have a choice, but it doesn't seem as though you have plenty of time to make it.

The cry of God and the trumpet in Zion are going out to everyone; the sad part is that only some will respond. Others will mock, judge, criticize, or just not pay any attention.

## TOGETHERNESS—TRUE FELLOWSHIP

*". . . I will put them together as the sheep of Bozrah, as the flock in the midst of their fold . . ."*

Micah 2:12

True fellowship in Christ is when true leadership and true followship work together in harmony. It's believers of one mind and one spirit all saying the same thing, not all playing together and frolicking in the sun or with our toys. Many of us love to eat. We really go for it. Many think it is true fellowship if we are centered around food.

True fellowship will be part of this revival, and we will get our enjoyment and satisfaction from healing the sick and from delivering bound people. Our joy will come from the results of our ministry in Christ.

I predict that goats and wolves will have nothing to do with the remnant. They will despise the order and authority in our ranks. This revival is for sheep. Hallelujah!

## LARGE CROWDS

*". . . they shall make great noise by reason of the multitude of men."*

Micah 2:12

I predict large crowds will bombard the local church. Many churches will be filled with new converts, and people will come craving God's touch on their lives.

The church will be noisy. Men and their families will come even from afar, and they will sing and shout unto God. Many will be found in the streets witnessing. People will be delivered. Shrieks will be heard when demons come out. The crippled and lame will be healed miraculously, and they will not restrain their praise.

## EVANGELISM EXPLOSION

Already in the flock that I pastor, over one hundred

souls were saved in ten days. Our people are reaching out, and they are touching others.

I predict a very large explosion in the field of evangelism. God is going to send hungry people to us asking us of the hope that lies within us. All we have to do is know how to answer them.

Answering hungry, questioning people is by far more productive than just scattering seed. Get ready. God is going to use you.

I see people running to God's house to get saved and delivered. We will be a most urgently-needed oasis in a troubled world.

## GOD MOVING SWIFTLY

*"Esaias also crieth concerning Israel, Though the number of the children of Israel be as the sand of the sea, a remnant shall be saved:*

*For he will finish the work, and cut it short in righteousness: because a short work will the Lord make upon the earth."*

Romans 9:27-28

Some people will say, "I'll stand back and watch this for a while. I'll just wait and see if it is God. I'll wait and see who its leaders will be."

I tell you, friends, this will come upon us so rapidly that it will overtake us.

God will execute His work quickly and thoroughly. Prepare now. I don't know how much time is left, but I do know it will be sufficient to climax the ages.

God is interested in using us to pull all things together. The Church is to be working with Christ on these things.

## LITTLE EFFORT—BIG RESULTS

*"Arise, shine; for thy light is come, and the glory of the LORD is risen upon thee.*

*For, behold, the darkness shall cover the earth, and gross darkness the people: but the LORD shall arise upon thee, and his glory shall be seen upon thee.*

*And the Gentiles shall come to thy light, and kings to the brightness of thy rising.*

*Lift up thine eyes round about, and see: all they gather themselves together, they come to thee: thy sons shall come from far, and thy daughters shall be nursed at thy side.*

*Then thou shalt see, and flow together, and thine heart shall fear, and be enlarged; because the abundance of the sea shall be converted unto thee, the forces of the Gentiles shall come unto thee.*

*The multitude of camels shall cover thee, the dromedaries of Midian and Ephah; all they from Sheba shall come: they shall bring gold and incense; and they shall shew forth the praises of the LORD."*

Isaiah 60:1-6

You won't have to muster up this one or go looking for it. God Himself is going to rise upon us. In the past, we have put in much effort to get little results, but I tell you the truth, in this wave of glory, we will use very little effort yet reap great results.

It will be God. Right in the midst of darkness, God will put His glory upon us.

Others will see it, and they will marvel at it. It won't come through doctrine or from others but strictly by divine impartation. It will be a sovereign ordination.

## ARISE, YOUR LIGHT HAS COME

Your light! That's right, the light and encouragement that we've been looking for will come. Not only will you aid others, but your gloom and despair will also be dismissed and sent away from you.

Hope and zeal will return to your life, and you will be fervent in spirit; that is, if you are numbered among the remnant.

## HIS FRUIT ON US

Thank God, we will finally bear forth His fruit. You can enjoy reading about it in Galatians 5:22-23. People will see His fruit in our lives. We Christians will look appetizing to many. We will be peculiar when we stand in the midst of the masses who will be consumed with the flesh. We will even enjoy ourselves and be thankful for the goodness of the Lord in our lives.

There will be no more prominent works of the flesh in the lives of the remnant believers.

## HIS GIFTS ON US

This also is glorious. We will have very few power

failures. In fact, we will have God's Holy Spirit working right beside us. Some of us enjoy this now.

In these final hours of Church history, God will wonderfully show up in answer to our prayers and in response to His name.

Men's hearts will tremble as prophecy is presented to them. Miracles will supersede the laws of nature and change people's destiny. Revelation knowledge will be released a word at a time, and many people will be helped.

It won't just happen in the pulpit or altar area. In fact, the greatest outpourings and manifestations will happen on your jobs, in your homes and yards, and in the midst of neighbors and relatives. Even in the streets, fairgrounds, and malls there will be a revival.

It will be a power surge. There has never been anything like it.

## HIS GLORY ON US

I can promise you this: People will know that we belong to Him. We will shine, and our countenance will be bright and cheerful. Pray for it, hunger for it, and chase after it. It is what the world needs. It is what you need.

## PEOPLE DRAWN TO US

*". . . They all gather together, they come to you. Your sons will come from afar, and your daughters will be carried in the arms."*

Isaiah 60:4 (NAS)

People you work with will begin to ask more questions. They will want to listen to you as you give them answers for the perplexities of their lives.

In many places, co-workers will meet together and come to you as a group asking you for help, direction, and definition for their lives.

Many of you will experience tremendous revival among your relatives. Some families will come together during holidays and reunions, and they will ask you to come and explain to them the way of the Lord. They will ask you to preach to them and pray for them.

They will come to us. God's glory on us will be like live bait on a clean hook. The fish will discover that it is not a man-made lure. Believe me, they will bite. You will catch!

## RADIANT AND REJOICING

Praise God for this. We will be radiant, and we will be rejoicing; that is, those numbered with the remnant. All others could be in deep trouble by now.

I can hardly wait to see God's people thrilled about His work. It is going to be so good to be able to see people totally enthused and full of zeal, running instead of walking, laughing instead of crying, working instead of playing.

We will rejoice everywhere, not just in church meetings. Everywhere Christians meet, they will send up hilarious praise.

## WEALTH COMES TO US

Wealth is coming to us—finally, praise God, and it

won't be unjust gain. It will come to us in ways that we will call miraculous. We will constantly testify of God's greatness. Our testimony will baffle the minds and schemes of the "used to be" rich. Institutions will come to the local church and to the believer looking for instructions and for some inside scoop. They will find no business propaganda, no schemes, no plans, no investors, and no gamblers but only believers who testify of God's great ability to provide.

Many ministries will have plenty of money and machinery, and their momentum will increase dramatically. It will be the most productive season that the Church has ever known.

God has spoken to many men and women of God to go and to do what He has instructed, but many have been discouraged, frustrated, and even failed because of lack of money. Lack of finances, machinery, personnel, and supply is probably the greatest weight that most ministries carry.

This will change! God is going to give us the supply we need. The spirits of poverty and lack will be bound from the ministry of Christ. Abundance and supply will be evident, and God's people will rejoice.

Now listen, I'm not talking about personal income as much as I am talking about church work income. God does want you personally to prosper but for the reason of propelling the gospel around the world. God will prosper you *so* you can prosper the church work.

I'm telling you that it's coming, friend. Get your stewardship and accounts ready for it. If your life and heart are sown into God's work, you qualify.

I encourage you to start now. Make sure your finances

are in order. Judge your stewardship, and reevaluate your budgets.

I encourage you to believe God for supply. Ask Him for encouragement in the ministry. He will oblige you. Just be sure you are believing Him for tools, not for toys. God always delivers tools to us more quickly than toys.

God wants the gospel preached to lost, suffering, and hurting humanity more than anything else in the universe.

# CHAPTER 7
# A REMNANT STORY

## ALMA LEE OWENS

Alma Lee Owens is a dear member of the church that I pastor. She was raised in denominationalism and remained there for 43 years. Finally, through a chain of events, she began to experience remnant satisfaction.

At the time of this writing, after waging the warfare of life, Alma Lee is 56 years old and is more powerful than ever before. She enjoys God's richest blessings as well as distributing them to others.

I've included here some excerpts from her autobiography that will show you a prime example of remnant material. Follow through the years to see the Holy Spirit line up Alma Lee for these end times:

1933-1934

I remember holiness tent meetings and the hot sawdust trails, with loud preaching and excited crowds. The Lord Jesus healed my Grandma Irish, and I would ask her to tell me again and again why there was a wheelchair and crutches in the attic. These experiences made a lasting impression in my heart as a child.

The depression of the '30s found us living together to survive. My dad tells of not being able to find 50 cents' worth of carpenter work a day. He fished the lakes for meat. We had no telephone, no electricity, and no indoor bathroom facilities.

1950-1957

I married Ray when he returned from a two-year stretch in the army. I thought being married and having my own child would bring fulfillment to my empty, boring life. I would often think, Is this all there is to life?

One day, as I cleaned and dusted my home, I looked at the black Bible I had been given in third grade at church (King James). I had tried to read it several times and could not understand. I kept thinking, I've got to find someone to help me understand what's in this book.

During my high school years and my '20s and '30s, my mom and dad were very involved with lodges—Eastern Stars, Masons, hunting and fishing, mammon, religion, and men's and ladies' meetings at our church. I remember feeling very angry at my parents because they had not introduced me to Jesus. I thought, I could have died and gone to hell, never knowing I was not saved!

I went to church faithfully and sang in the choir, just like other people around me. My hunger was great.

My Born-Again Experience

In 1957, a retreat was scheduled at St. Mary's Lake near Battle Creek, Michigan. I had never heard of this man who was to speak, but I thought it would be fun to get away with my friends for a weekend. I was so hungry, I soaked up every word.

He made God's word so easy and simple to understand. I sat at the lunch table next to this man at break on Saturday. I asked him if he would come to Clare and teach our people these things. He paused and said, "I don't know if I can, but what are you going to do about it?" I said, "Well, I have everything written down right here, and, if I can remember everything, I'm going back to Clare to tell everyone who will listen to me what you've taught me." He smiled and placed his hand on my head and said, "God bless you, my dear."

God began to pour out that blessing, and fire and heat like hot blood slowly began to flow through my body, from my head to my toes. I knew it was God, but I didn't understand what was happening to me. My clothes were soaked, and I felt like I was in a different dimension. I stood up, embarrassed. The room was filled with a heavy, gray-like fog, so thick I could have cut it with a knife and left a hole in it. I slowly made my way alone up the stairs and outside. When I felt the fresh air on my skin, I never felt so whole or so healed. I knew it was God; I felt like hollering and screaming and running and jumping. My mind kept saying, You've got to calm down. I didn't know what to do. I stayed by myself for some time. I knew I was different but didn't understand. I later told the ladies I was with what happened, and one said, "Glory to God, you are the one; you are the one we have been praying for. You got saved, you got saved!"

I felt such an awesome presence upon me. I hardly knew what to do. I wept and wept, feeling the responsibility. I was 27 years old with an unsaved husband and two children. The Scriptures were opened up to me, and I could understand. It seemed every prayer I prayed was answered. I spent every moment I could reading my Bible and praying.

There was a mark that appeared on my forehead like a skin burn about 1″ x 3″. It lasted a week or so. To this day, I don't know what it was. It was not sore.

The people in my church did not know what to think of me—overboard, fanatic, carried away. They even said, "Oh, she will get over it." But I never did. Jesus just kept getting sweeter. I had a nine-month "high" before I leveled off.

1968

We were invited to counsel at a Methodist senior high youth camp at Lake Louise in Northern Michigan. We learned later that much planning, pre-prayer, fasting, and careful selection of staff had gone into this camp. The pastor and dean were Charismatic, but many others were not (about 150 to 175 in all).

Lunchtime on Monday, after our Sunday arrival, found it pouring rain. As we were getting acquainted and making introductions, I soon noticed a girl, Mona, at my table. She was full of life, and I asked her to tell me how she met Jesus and how she became baptized in the Holy Ghost. I soon could see the benefits of her coming down to my cabin and telling her story to my 20 girls. So she came, and they were all ears! Then I asked Mona if she would pray for me to get the "deluxe job" baptism of the Holy Spirit.

After her laying on of hands, we prayed. Nothing appeared to happen to me, but my assistant began to pray in tongues, then another girl and another. We just sat there and watched as the Holy Ghost fell first on one, then another. Crying and sobs, joy and laughter, all at the same time. The girls ran out in the rain to tell others in nearby cabins. Some ran to the chapel. The altar was filled with young people crying out to God and utterances in the Spirit. Some even began to prophesy. Others were speaking in oriental languages.

I spent my time going from one to another, laughing and crying with them. Some were even slain in the Spirit that week. I began to notice people standing at the back of the chapel. The religious crowd had arrived—glaring at us—no smiles either! On the path next to the lake in the woods, as the rain ran down my umbrella, the question came to me, "Are you going to seek after this experience?" And the words came, "If you do, your husband will divorce you."

1969-1970

Upon returning from camp, I visited a lady in Clare who was known to be Pentecostal. She shared much with me and gave me a set of books by Gordon Lindsay on the gifts of the Spirit. I read everything I could find. A hornet's nest was being stirred up against us. Other adults were being baptized in the Holy Ghost and now other youth from the Clare area too. It was almost useless for the kids to go to church and Sunday school because of the ridicule and scoffers. We were of the devil, they said.

I was forced out of my Sunday school class, blackballed from the Evangelism Commission, and was watched. I was not even asked to sing much in later years. I knew God had something better in mind. I kept looking.

1970s

Praying and waiting for a place to go where people would just love Jesus and each other and practice what the Bible teaches, I'd say, "Oh, Jesus, You didn't give me this gift of music and this voice and this glory in my heart for me to suffocate and die in this place." But I stayed because there was nothing else.

Divorce, sin, immorality, and gossip riddled the church over and over. I wondered why someone didn't do something to stop it. It seemed looking respectable on the outside was more important than being clean on the inside.

November 1980

On my birthday, Thursday, November 15, 1980, I came to Midland to spend a few days with a friend. She began to tell me about a Word of Faith preacher who had just come to start a new church in Midland. She said the gifts of the Spirit were tremendous, and I must come and hear him. So we went to the meeting at a school. I liked what I heard. I knew it was God for me. All I can say is my heart just kept on saying, "Yes, yes; that's it; that's it!" I began to realize bit by bit, month by month, year by year, how great God is and what a great thing He was doing in our midst and, once again, I was in it.

I was still searching for help for my husband, myself, and our marriage. I had hoped the men in this church would be able to help him. The denominational church we had been attending was dead. I resigned there and joined Living Word. My husband came off and on, but soon he announced he was leaving and wanted to just live alone the rest of his life.

The words of your assistant rang in my ears. "I don't know how, Mrs. Owens, but you are a woman of God, and God is going to see that you are taken care of." The prophecies, sermons, and scriptures Pastor Mark preached literally saved my life. No matter how desperate the external condition of my life was, God's hand, His love, His light were stronger and brighter. They anchored my soul in peace. An awesome presence was wrapped around us. I took advantage of every altar service I could.

And so, I left 50 years of my life behind and came March 15, 1985, to Midland and Living Word Outreach Center, my new home, to be with people I really hardly knew. They were God's people, God's remnant.

Now I'm on a new quest for remnant material with Dr. Barclay and Living Word Church. We are seeking out the new wave of God's Spirit together.

## A WORD ABOUT ALMA LEE

I'm so proud of Alma Lee and all the many Christians like her who serve with me. One of the greatest blessings of any pastor is to see fruit appear on the believers they lead and feed.

If you are a sheep, be the best one you can possibly be. Go for all of what God has.

You'll be constantly amazed that He will do even more than what you ask or think. Nothing is too great for God to do on your behalf.

There is no greater feeling than to have God touching your life. The touch of God is so dynamic and so sweet that it melts our hearts. It keeps us in His perfect will. It stirs up our love.

Just like this story of Alma Lee Owens, you can have your own story—a story that shows forth the praises of God, a story that testifies of His magnificent works.

There is no better feeling than that of looking back and knowing God had His hand upon you and that He has been guiding you year after year after year. What a beautiful track record—God bringing you from glory to glory and from faith to faith.

## YOU'RE WRITING A BOOK

Did you know you are writing a book? That's right. Each and every hour of your life you are making records. The angels are watching and witnessing. The Holy Spirit is walking with you. Even the devil and his army are taking note of what you are up to.

Realize it! You are making history. You are now laying up treasures in Heaven. You and I both will give an account for our stewardship, our actions, and yes, even every idle word that we have spoken. All of our works will be judged and tried by fire. We will all know if we have stored up gold, silver, and precious stones or wood, hay, and stubble.

What you do now, you will be held accountable for. Even your leaders will have to give an account for your soul. I think a lot of us lose track of this.

The book will be opened. The Book of Life and all the other chronicles of Heaven will be opened. You and your acts (both good and bad) will be opened. Your life will be reviewed, at least from the time you were born again.

Realize it. Everything you say and do is being set in record as your earthly history. Go, man, go. Go, woman, go. Do those mighty exploits. Perform those courageous tasks. Conquer those opposing forces. Overcome the devil's war against you. Store up treasures in Heaven. Bear forth all the fruit you can. Move in every gift you can. Be powerful in God. Be awesome. Be a terrible threat to God's enemies. Be holy and upright. Be of a contrite and broken spirit. God will honor your life!

# A PRAYER FOR YOU

My prayer for you is:

*". . . grant unto thy servants, that with all boldness they may speak thy word,*

*By stretching forth thine hand to heal; and that signs and wonders may be done by the name of thy holy child Jesus."*

Acts 4:29-30

Heavenly Father, I beseech You in Jesus' name, that You would cause each of us to grow in the character of our being. Help us to be more pleasing to You than we ever have been. Help us to speak boldly, yet in season. Help us to tell the truth and be what You want us to be.

Dear Lord, please melt away our facades and help us to stop playing games. Help each of us to see the Kingdom of God as the priority and not our own kingdom.

We are going to have backbone, Lord, in our servant-hood to You and our witness to the world.

We love You, Lord. Thank You for answering this prayer, Sir!

# Books by Mark T. Barclay

## Beware of Seducing Spirits

This is not a book on demonology. It is a book about the misbehavior of men and women and the seducing and deceiving spirits that influence them to do what they do. Brother Barclay exposes the most prominent seducing spirits of the last days.

## Beware of the Sin of Familiarity

This book is a scriptural study on the most devastating sin in the Body of Christ today. The truths in this book will make you aware of this excess familiarity and reveal to you some counterattacks.

## Building a Supernatural Church

A guide to pioneering, organizing, and establishing a new local church. This is a fast-reading, simple, instructional guide to leaders and helps people who are working together to build the Church.

## Charging the Year 2000

This book will remind you of the last-days' promises of God as well as alert you to the many snares and falsehoods with which satan will try to deceive and seduce last-days' believers. "A handbook for living in the '90s."

## Enduring Hardness

God has called His Church an army and the believers soldiers. It is mandatory that all Christians endure hardness as good soldiers of Jesus Christ. This book will help build more backbone in you.

## How to Always Reap a Harvest

In this book Brother Barclay explains the principles that make believers successful and fruitful. It shows you how to live a better life and become far more productive and enjoy a full harvest.

## How to Avoid Shipwreck

A book of preventive medicine, helping people stay strong and full of faith. You will be strengthened by this book as you learn how to anchor your soul.

## How to Relate to Your Pastor

It is very important in these last days that God's people understand the office of pastor. As we put into practice these principles, the Church will grow in numbers and also increase its vision for the world.

## Improving Your Performance

Every Christian everywhere needs to read this book. Even leaders will be challenged by this writing. It will help tremendously in the organization and unity of your ministry and working force.

## The Making of a Man of God

In this book you'll find some of the greatest, yet simplest, insights to becoming a man or woman of God and to launching your ministry with accuracy and credibility. The longevity of your ministry will be enhanced by the truths herein. You will learn the difference between being a convert, an epistle, a disciple, and a minister.

## Preachers of Righteousness

This is not a book for pulpiteers or reverends only but for all of us. It reveals the real ministry style of Jesus Christ and the sold-out commitment of His followers— the most powerful, awesome force on the face of the earth.

### The Real Truth About Tithing
This book is a thorough study of God's Word on tithing, which will fully inform believers how to tithe biblically and accurately. You will be armed with the truth, and your life will never be the same!

### The Remnant Church
God has always had a people and will always have a people. Brother Barclay speaks of the upcoming revival and how we can be those who are alive and remain when our Master returns.

### Sheep, Goats, and Wolves
A scriptural yet practical explanation of human behavior in our local churches and how church leaders and members can deal with each other. You will especially enjoy the tests that are in the back of this book.

### The Sin of Lawlessness
Lawlessness always challenges authority and ultimately is designed to hurt people. This book will convict those who are in lawlessness and warn those who could be future victims. It will help your life and straighten your walk with Him.

### Six Ways to Check Your Leadings
It seems that staying in the main flow of Jesus is one of the most difficult things for believers to do, and I'm including some preachers. Many people border on mysticism and a world of fantasy. God is not a goofy God. He doesn't intend for His people to be goofy either. This book reveals the six most valuable New Testament ways to live in accuracy and stay perfectly on course. This book is a must for living in the '90s.

### Warring Mental Warfare
Every person is made up of body, soul, and spirit and fights battles on each of these three fronts. The war against your soul (made up of your mind, will, and emotions) is real and as lethal as spiritual and natural enemies. This book will help you identify, war against, and defeat the enemies of your soul. Learn to quit coping with depression, anxiety, fear, and other hurts and begin conquering them now!

### What About Death?
This book deals with the enemy, death, and how to overcome it. Brother Barclay also explains what the Bible says about life after death. I have found that many people have no real biblical knowledge on this subject and therefore are unsure about it all the days of their lives.

### Basic Christian Handbook (mini book)
This mini book is packed full of scriptures and basic information needed for a solid Christian foundation. It would make an inexpensive and effective tract and is a must for new converts. Many church workers are using it for altar counseling.

### The Captain's Mantle (mini book)
Something happened in the cave Adullum. Find out how 400 distressed, indebted, and discontented men came out of that cave as one of the most awesome armies in history.

### Have You Seen This Person Lately? (mini book)
Did you once serve the Lord actively and fervently but now you have cooled off some? Are you now serving Him and want to assure that you will never backslide? Do you have family or friends who are backslidden or unchurched? Then this book is for you! Its contents will help you find your way home.